*This journal contains
the daily thoughts of*

_____

_____

Date

*"I know the plans I have for
you," declares the L*ORD,
*"plans to prosper you and not
to harm you, plans to give
you hope and a future."*

Jeremiah 29:11

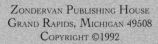

ZONDERVAN PUBLISHING HOUSE
GRAND RAPIDS, MICHIGAN 49508
COPYRIGHT ©1992

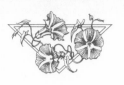

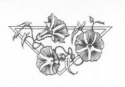

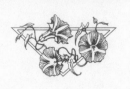

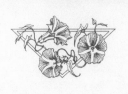

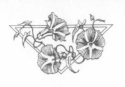

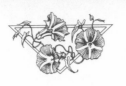

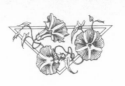

Charm is

deceptive, and

beauty is fleeting;

but a woman who

fears the LORD is

to be praised.

Proverbs 31:30